Ready for School

We Sh

Sharon Gordon

Marshall Cavendish
Benchmark
New York

We like to share.

We share desks.

We like to share.

We share toys.

We like to share.

We share snacks.

We like to share.

We share books.

We like to share.

We share crayons.

We like to share.

We share seats.

We like to share.

We share swings.

We like to share.

We share friends.

We like to share!

We Share

books

crayons

desks

friends

seats

snacks

swings

toys

Index

Page numbers in **boldface** are illustrations.

About the Author

Sharon Gordon has written many books for young children. She has always worked as an editor. Sharon and her husband Bruce have three children, Douglas, Katie, and Laura, and one spoiled pooch, Samantha. They live in Midland Park, New Jersey.

With thanks to Nanci Vargus, Ed.D. and
Beth Walker Gambro, reading consultants

Marshall Cavendish
99 White Plains Road
Tarrytown, New York 10591-9001
www.marshallcavendish.us

Library of Congress Cataloging-in-Publication Data

Gordon, Sharon.
We share / by Sharon Gordon.— 1st ed.
p. cm. — (Bookworms. Ready for school)
Summary: "Demonstrates the importance of sharing with others at school"—Provided by publisher.
Includes index.
ISBN 978-0-7614-3276-0 (PB)
ISBN 0-7614-1993-4 (HB)
1. Sharing—Juvenile literature. 2. School children—Conduct of life—Juvenile literature. I. Title. II. Series.

BJ1533.G4G67 2005
177'.7—dc22
2005002082

Photo Research by Anne Burns Images

Cover Photo by Corbis/Ted Horowitz

The photographs in this book are used with permission and through the courtesy of:
Corbis: pp. 1, 3, 19, 20 (bottom r) Ariel Skelley; pp. 7, 21 (bottom r) Ed Bock; pp. 9, 13, 20 (top r),
21 (top r) Jose Luis Pelaez, Inc.; pp. 11, 15, 17, 20 (top l), 21 (top l), 21 (bottom l) Tom & Dee Ann McCarthy.
SuperStock: pp. 5, 20 (bottom l) age footstock.

Printed in Malaysia
1 3 5 6 4 2